CUSTOMS OF LORRAINE

Louis VII
King of France

Translated by: D.P. Curtin

Copyright @ 2006 Dalcassian Publishing Company

All rights reserved. No part of this publication may be reproduced, distributed, or transmitted in any form or by any means, including photocopying, recording, or other electronic or mechanical methods, without the prior written permission of the publisher, except in the case of brief quotations embodied in critical reviews and certain other non-commercial uses permitted by copyright law. For permission request, write to Dalcassian Publishing Company at dalcassianpublishing at gmail.com

ISBN: 979-8-8693-5515-7 (Paperback)

Library of Congress Control Number:
Author: Curtin, D.P. (1985-)

Printed by Ingram Content Group, 1 Ingram Blvd, La Vergne, Tennessee

First printing edition 2006.

CUSTOMS OF LORRAINE

CHARTER OF FRENCH LORRAINE

This is the charter of King Louis of Lorraine

Louis, et cetera. Let it be known to all present and future that:

1. Whoever has a house in the parish of Lorraine, for his house, and for a certain parcel of land, if he has it in the same parish, he shall pay a tax of six denarii only; and if he has acquired it, let him hold it for the tax of his house.

2. No man of the parish of Lorraine shall return a tonle nor any custom for his nourishment; nor shall he make a threat concerning his goods, or his labor, or the labor of his people, whatever animals he may have; and he shall never return the fodder for his wine, which he had from his servants.

3. Let none of them go on an expedition or ride, unless they return to their home that day, if they will.

CUSTOMS OF LORRAINE

4. And none of them shall pay the toll as far as Stampas, nor as far as Aurelianos, nor as far as Miliacum, which is in the village of Gastinense, nor as far as Meledunum (Milan).

5. And whoever has property in the parish of Lorraine, shall lose nothing of it for whatever he has done, unless he has done it against us or one of our guests.

6. No one coming or returning to the holiday or to the market of Lorriane shall be arrested or disturbed unless he has committed the crime on that day. And no one on the day of the market or slaying in Lorraine should take of his pledge, except on the same day as that pledge was made.

7. And the forfeit of sixty solidi should come to five solidi, and the forfeit of five solidi should come to twelve denarii; and the cry of the presbyter to four pence.

8. And let none of them go out of Lorriane to plead with the lord the king.

9. No one, neither we nor anyone else, should make a cut, or a removal, or a request to the people of Lorriane.

10. And no one of the Lorraine should sell wine with the edict, except the king, who sells his own wine in his cellar.

11 And Lorraine will have credit in food to pay our and the king's work for a full fifteen days. And if any one has the bail of the king's lord or any other, he shall not hold it for more than eight days, unless of his own accord.

12. And if another commits mischief against another, without breaching a castle or a burg, and agreeing with a cry that has not been made in advance, he is not on this account to make amends to us or to our leader; they paid the district

by; and if one makes a complaint about another, and the other makes no amends towards the other, he will make no amends for us or for our superior.

13. And if someone else should have performed the sacrament, it is permissible for him to forgive.

14. And if the men of Lorriacus have given the fords of a duel at random, and, with the approval of the governor, have agreed before the hostages are given, each of them shall pay two solidi and six denarii; and if hostages have been given, each of them shall pay seven shillings and sixpence. And if the duel was between legitimate men, the hostages of the vanquished shall pay one hundred and twelve solidos.

15. None of them will make a Corvata for us, except once a year to bring the Aurelians our wine; nor will others do this except those who have had horses and teams, and have been summoned thence, nor will they have agency from us. And the peasants will bring wood for our kitchen.

16. None of them should be held captive if he could give a pledge to come to justice.

17. And every one of them, if he wishes to sell, shall sell his possessions, and with the proceeds of the sales, if he wishes to depart from the town, he shall depart free and in peace, unless he has committed a crime in the town.

18. And whoever has remained in the parish of Lorraine for a year and a day, following him with no clamor, nor by us or by a superior, has hindered his righteousness, may he remain free and quiet thenceforth.

19. And no one will plead with anyone except for the sake of receiving and executing righteousness.

20. And when men go from Lorriaco to the Aurelians with trade, they shall pay only a coin for their team on the way out of the city, that is to say, when they go there is no reason to strike. And when they went to Marcius for the cause, they paid forty-four denarii for the team on the way out to Aurelian, and two denarii on the way in.

21. At the weddings in Lorraine, he will have nothing to pray for, nor will he have an attendant.

22. And no farmer in a parish land in Lorriane who cultivates the land with a plow should give more than one mina of rye to all the servants of Lorriane, as is customary, when the harvest is due.

23. And if any soldier or servant finds horses or other animals belonging to the people of Lorriaco in our forests, he must not take them except to the governor of Lorriaco. And if any animal from the parish of Lorraine enters our forest, driven away by bulls or forced by flies, or by a shark, he shall not have to pay the guardians anything for that reason. And if he knowingly enters with someone guarding him, he will give 12 denarii for him; and if there be more, he shall pay the same amount for each.

24. In the furnaces of Lorraine there will not be the usual porters.

25. And the guard will not be the custom of Lorraine.

26. And a man from Lorriane, if he takes his salt or wine to the Aurelians, will give only one penny per team.

27. And no one of the men of Lorraine owes reparation to the governor of Stampari, nor to the governor of Piver, nor to the whole of Gastines.

28. None of them will give a ton to Ferrari, nor Castronantone, nor Puteoli, nor Nibelle.

29. And the men of Lorriane shall take the dead forest for their own use outside the forest.

30. And whoever buys or sells something in the Lorraine market and through forgetfulness retains his tonle, he shall pay it after eight days, without any reason, if he can swear that he did not knowingly withhold it.

31. And none of the people of Lorria having a house or a vineyard or a meadow or a field or any building in the land of St. Benedict shall justify himself as the abbot of St. Benedict or as his servant, unless he has sheared for the sheaf, or for his census; and then he will not leave Lorriacus for the sake of holding on to righteousness.

32. And if any of the men of Lorriane be accused of anything, and cannot be proved by a witness, he shall acquit himself by his own hand, against the evidence of the applicant.

33. Nor shall any one of the same parish sell or buy anything during the week, and whatever he buys on Wednesday in the market, he shall give no custom for his own use.

34. Now these customs, as they were granted to the people of Lorriane, are likewise common to the people who live at Corpalez and at Chantelou and in the bailiwick of Herpard.

35. Accordingly, we decided that every time the prefect moved in the village, one after the other would swear that he would strictly observe these customs, and likewise the new servants, whenever they moved.

LATIN TEXT

CARTA FRANCHESIE LORRIACI

Hec est carta Ludovici regis de Lorriaco.

Ludovicus, etc. Notum sit omnibus presentibus et futuris quod:

1. Quicumque in Lorriaci parrochia domum habebit, pro domo sua, et pro quodam arpenno terre, si in eadem parrochia habuerit, sex denarios census tantum persolvat; et, si illud acquisierit, ad censum domus sue illud teneat.

2. Nullus hominum de parrochia Lorriaci tonleium neque aliquam consuetudinem reddat de nutritura sua; nec etiam de annona sua quam de labore suo vel de labore suorum quorumcumque animalium habuerit minagium reddat; et de vino suo quod de niveis suis habuerit foragium nunquam reddat.

3. Nullus eorum in expeditionem nec equitacionem eat, nisi ea dem die ad domum suam, si voluerit, reveniat.

4. Et nullus eorum pedagium usque Stampas reddat, nec usque Aurelianos, nec usque Miliacum, quod est in pago Gastinensi, nec usque Meledunum.

5. Et quicumque in parrochia Lorriaci possessionem suam habuerit, nihil ex ea perdat pro quocumque forifacto, nisi adversum nos vel aliquem de hospi tibus nostris forifecerit.

6. Nullus ad ferias seu ad mercatum Lorriaci veniens seu rediens capiatur nec disturbetur, nisi die illa forifactum fecerit. Et nullus in die mercati vel ferie Lorriaci vadium plegii sui capiat, nisi die consimili plegiacio illa facta fuerit.

7. Et forifactum de LX solidis ad quinque solidos, et forifactum de quinque solidis ad XII denarios veniat; et clamor prepositi ad IIII denarios.

8. Et nullus eorum a Lorriaco cum domino rege placitaturus exeat.

9. Nullus, nec nos nec alius, hominibus de Lorriaco talliam, nec ablationem, nec rogam faciat.

10. Et nullus Lorriaci vinum cum edicto vendat, excepto rege qui proprium vinum in cellario suo vendat.

11 Lorriaci autem habebimus creditionem in cibis ad nostrum et regine opus ad dies quindecim completes persolvendum. Et si quis vadium domini regis vel alius habuerit, non tenebit ultra octo dies, nisi sponte.

12. Et, si alius erga alium ini miciciam incurrerit, absque castelli vel burgi infractura, et clamore pre posito non facto concordaverit, nichil ob hoc nobis nec preposito nostro sit emendaturus, et, si clamor inde factus fuerit, licet illis concordare, ex quo districtum per solverint; et, si alius de alio clamorem fecerit, et alter erga al terum nullam fecerit emendationem, nihil pro his nobis aut preposito nostro eritemendaturus.

13. Et si alius alii facere sacramentum debuerit condonare ei liceat.

14. Et si homines de Lorriaco vadia duelli temere dederint, et, prepositi assensu, antequam tribuantur obsides, concordaverint, duos solidos et VI denarios persolvat uterque; et, si obsides dati fuerint, VII solidos et sex denarios persolvat uterque. Et si de legitimis hominibus duellum factum fuerit, obsides de victi C et XII solidos persolvent.

15. Eorum nullus corvatam nobis faciet, nisi semel in anno ad vinum nostrum adducendum Aurelianos; nec alii hoc facient nisi illi qui equos et quadrigas

habuerint, et inde summoniti fuerint, nec a nobis habebunt procurationem. Villani autem ligna ad coquinam nostram adducent.

16. Nullus eorum captus teneatur si plegium veniendi ad jus dare potuerit.

17. Et eorum quilibet res suas, si vendere voluerit, vendat, et redditis venditionibus, a villa, si recedere voluerit, liber et quietus recedat, nisi in villa forifactum fecerit.

18. Et quicumque in parrochia Lorriaci anno et die manserit, nullo clamore eum sequente, neque per nos sive per prepositum rectitudinem prohibuerit, deinceps liber et quietus permaneat.

19. Et nullus cum aliquo placitabit nisi causa rectitudinis recipiende et exequende.

20. Et quando homines de Lorriaco ibunt Aurelianos cum mercatura, pro quadriga sua solum nummum persolvent in urbis egressu, scilicet quando ibunt non causa ferie. Et, quando causa ferie in Marcio ierint, in egressu Aurelianis IIII denarios persolvent pro quadriga, et in ingressu II denarios.

21. In nupciis Lorriaci preco consuetudine nichil habebit, nec excubitor.

22. Et nullus agricola de parrochia Lorriaci qui terram colat cum aratro plusquam unam minam siliginis omnibus de Lorriaco servientibus consuetudinem prebeat, quando messis erit.

23. Et si miles aliquis, seu servions, equos vel alia animalia hominum de Lorriaco in nemoribus nostris invenerit, non debet illa ducere nisi ad prepositum de Lorriaco. Et, si aliquod animal de parrochia Lorriaci forestam nostram, a tauris fugatum vel a muscis coactum intraverit sive haiam, nichil ideo debebit prepositis emen dare ille cujus fuerit animal qui poterit jurare

quod custode invito illud intraverit. Et si, aliquo custodiente scienter, intraverit, XII denarios pro illo dabit; et, si plura fuerint, totidem pro quolibet persolvat.

24. In furnis Lorriaci non erunt portatores consuetudine.

25. Et excubie non erunt Lorriaci consuetudine.

26. Et aliquis de Lorriaco, si duxerit sal vel vinum suum Aurelianos, pro quadriga I denarium dabit tantum.

27. Et nullus hominum Lorriaci debet emendationem preposito Stamparum, nec preposito Piveris, nec in toto Gastinesio.

28. Nullus eorum dabit tonleium Ferrariis, nec Castronantone, nec Puteolis, nec Nibelle.

29. Et homines de Lorriaco nemus mortuum ad usum suum extra forestam capiant.

30. Et quicumque in mercato Lorriaci emerit aliquid vel vendiderit et per oblivionem tonleium suum retinuerit, post octo dies illud persolvet, sine aliqua causa, si jurare poterit quod scienter non retinuisset.

31. Et nullus hominum Lorriaci habentium domum vel vineam vel pratum aut agrum vel ediflcium aliquod in terra Sancti Benedicti justificabit se pro abbate Sancti Benedicti vel pro ejus serviente, nisi pro garba, vel pro censu suo forifecerit; et tunc a Lorriaco non exibit causa rectitudinis tenende.

32. Et, si aliquis hominum de Lorriaco accusatus de aliquo fuerit, et teste comprobari non poterit, contra probationem impetentis per solam manum suam se deculpabit.

33. Nullus etiam de eadem parrochia de quoeumque vendiderit vel emerit super septimanam, et de quocumque emerit in die Mercurii in mercato pro usu suo nullam consuetudinem dabit.

34. Hec autem consuetudines, sicut concesse sunt hominibus de Lorriaco, similiter communes sunt hominibus qui habitant apud Corpalez et apud Chantelou et in balliata Herpardi.

35. Proinde constituimus ut quotiens in villa movebitur prepositus, unus post alterum juret se stabiliter servaturum has consuetudines, et similiter novi servientes, quotiens movebuntur.

The Scriptorium Project is the work of a small group of lay people of various apostolic churches who are interested in the preservation, transmission, and translation of the works of the early and medieval church. Our efforts are to make the works of the church fathers accessible to anyone who might have an interest in Christian antiquities and the theological, philosophical, and moral writings that have become the bedrock of Western Civilization.

To-date, our releases have pulled from the Greek, Syriac, Georgian, Latin, Celtic, Ethiopian, and Coptic traditions of Christianity, and have been pulled from sundry local traditions and languages.

Other Selections from the Early Frankish Church Series:

Frankish Royal Elections: Boso, Eudes, Louis, & Guy (Sept. 2005)
Chapters by Carloman II, King of West Francia (Dec. 2005)
Chapters for France & Aquitaine by Charles II the Bald (Feb. 2006)
Customs of Lorraine by Louis VII, King of France (May 2006)
Roman Laws of Burgundy by Gondomar II, King of Burgundy (Sept. 2006)
Apology to Hugh & Robert, Kings of France by St. Abbo of Fleury (Nov. 2006)
Frankish & Visigothic Councils: 549-615 AD (June 2007)
Acts of the Synod of of Reims by Pope Sylvester II (Aug. 2010)
Letter to Brunhilda of Austrasia by St. Germain of Paris (Sept. 2010)
The Spiritual Combat by St. Bernard of Clairvaux (Dec. 2010)
In Praise of the New Chivalry by St. Bernard of Clairvaux (Jan. 2011)
Testament by St. Burgundofara the Abbess (Jan. 2016)
Laws of the Monastery and the Church by Theuderic III, King of Franks (Feb. 2016)
The Life of King Sigebert II by Sigebert of Gembloux (Mar. 2016)
Two Letters from a Gallic Patrician by Dynamius the Patrician (July 2016)
Life of St. Germain by St. Venantius Fortunatus (Aug. 2016)
Three Letters from the Companion of the Bulgars by St. Rupert of Juvavum (Aug. 2017)
An Account of the Gallican Liturgy by St. Germain of Paris (June 2018)
Preludes by Photius of Paris (Nov. 2018)
The Privileges of Rome by Louis I the Pious, Frankish Emperor (Apr. 2019)
Edicts of the Synod of Paris by Chlothar II, King of Franks (Aug. 2019)
Laws of the Church by Chlothar III, King of Franks (Apr. 2020)
Laws of the Church by St. Dagobert II, King of Franks (Sept. 2020)
Letters of Paulinus by St. Paulinus of Aquileia (Aug. 2021)
The Italian Diplomas by Charlemagne, Holy Roman Emperor (Apr. 2023)

www.ingramcontent.com/pod-product-compliance
Lightning Source LLC
LaVergne TN
LVHW051924060526
838201LV00060B/4166